GARETH STEVENS
VITAL SCIENCE
Earth Science

EARTH'S RESOURCES

by Alfred J. Smuskiewicz
Science curriculum consultant: Suzy Gazlay, M.A.,
science curriculum resource teacher

GARETH**STEVENS**
GS PUBLISHING
A Member of the WRC Media Family of Companies

Please visit our web site at: www.garethstevens.com
For a free color catalog describing Gareth Stevens Publishing's
list of high-quality books and multimedia programs, call
1-800-542-2595 (USA) or 1-800-387-3178 (Canada).
Gareth Stevens Publishing's fax: (414) 332-3567.

Library of Congress Cataloging-in-Publication Data

Smuskiewicz, Alfred J.
    Earth's resources / Alfred J. Smuskiewicz.
        p. cm. — (Gareth Stevens vital science - earth science)
    Includes bibliographical references and index.
    ISBN-13: 978-0-8368-7763-2 (lib. bdg.)
    ISBN-13: 978-0-8368-7874-5 (softcover)
    1. Natural resources—Juvenile literature. I. Title.
    HC85.S59   2007
    333.7—dc22   2006033116

This edition first published in 2007 by
Gareth Stevens Publishing
A Member of the WRC Media Family of Companies
330 West Olive Street, Suite 100
Milwaukee, WI 53212 USA

Produced by White-Thomson Publishing Ltd.
Editor: Clare Collinson
Designer: Clare Nicholas
Photo researcher/commissioning editor: Stephen White-Thomson
Gareth Stevens editorial direction: Mark Sachner
Gareth Stevens editor: Leifa Butrick
Gareth Stevens art direction: Tammy West
Gareth Stevens production: Jessica Yanke and Robert Kraus

Science curriculum consultant: Tom Lough, Ph.D., Associate Professor of Science Education, Murray State
University, Murray, Kentucky

Illustrations by Peter Bull Art Studio
Photo credits: CORBIS, pp. 5t (© Tom Stewart), 5b (Roy Morsch), 8 (© John Hicks), 27 (© Ted Spiegel),
28 (© M. ou Me. Desjeux, Bernard), 31 (© Colin Keates), 34 (© Vasily Fedosenko/Reuters); Ecoscene,
p. 45; Geoscience, p. 15 (all); © iStockphoto.com, pp. 6 (Oleg Kozlov), 10 (Therese McKeon), 12 (Steve
Mcsweeny) , 13 (Valerie Loiseleux), 16l (Jillian Pond), 16r (Lisa F. Young), 17 (Damir Spanic), title page
and 19 (Norbert Rohr), 20 (Ivan Stevanovic), 21 (Steve Geer), 22 (Jeffrey Zavitski), 24 (Tracy Tucker),
26 (Tanja-Tiziana Burdi), 29 (Tomasz Resiak), cover and 30 (Andrew Penner), 32 (Magdalena Kucova),
33 (Magdalena Kucova), 35 (Bill Grove), 37 (Christoph Ermel), 39 (Mark Weiss), 41 (Laurence Gough),
42 (Tore Johannesen); Science Photo Library p. 11 (NASA).

Cover: A pump jack, or "nodding donkey," such as this one in Alberta, Canada, drives a pump that is
located deep in an underground oil reservoir.
Title page: At the Janubio saltworks on the island of Lanzarote, in the Canary Islands, salt is produced by
the evaporation of seawater in the heat of the Sun.

Printed in Canada

1 2 3 4 5 6 7 8 9 10 10 09 08 07 06

TABLE OF CONTENTS

① INTRODUCTION

The natural resources of Earth—such as air, water, rocks and minerals, soil, and plant and animal life—provide human beings with everything they need to live. Every human activity uses one or more of Earth's natural resources—even activities that you hardly ever think about, such as breathing. Each breath you take uses one of Earth's most abundant resources—air. Every time you take a bath or shower, you are using another abundant resource—water. Turning on a lamp, talking on the telephone, riding in a car, eating a meal—each of these activities uses Earth's natural resources.

Population Pressures

You use so many natural resources each and every day that it may not occur to you that these resources may not always be around. Remember—you are not the only one using these resources! There are more than 500 million other people in North America—and approximately 6.5 billion people throughout the world. These people all use natural resources—for food, fuel, electrical power, building materials, clothes, cars, computers, and countless other needs.

The population of the world is growing each year at an average rate of about 1.2 percent, and the number of people in some parts of the world is growing much faster than that. As Earth becomes home to more and more people, the supplies of some of its natural resources are getting smaller and smaller.

Earth's Natural Resources Will Not Last Forever

Some natural resources are limited and, if people keep using them, they may eventually be used up. These nonrenewable resources include fossil fuels, such as petroleum (crude oil), natural gas, and coal, which we use to produce our electricity and power our vehicles. The metals copper, lead, nickel, and zinc are also nonrenewable resources.

Other natural resources exist in unlimited amounts or in amounts that can be easily replaced. These renewable resources include air, water, sunlight, wind, and plants and animals.

Conservation Is Crucial

To help ensure that humanity does not run out of the resources it needs, we all must learn to use Earth's natural resources more wisely. Conservation of natural resources means using what we need, without wasting the resources or using more than we need. This is a difficult lesson to learn, especially in the Western world, where we have long taken resources for granted. But if we use fewer nonrenewable resources, and if we find the most efficient ways to use all resources, it is more likely that future generations will inherit the bounty that nature has provided us.

You use Earth's natural resources every day, often without giving them a second thought. The water that you sprinkle on the lawn—or have fun playing with—and the wind that lifts your kite skyward are two kinds of natural resources. ▼ ▶

2 EARTH'S NATURAL RESOURCES

Life would not be possible without the resources we find in nature. Throughout history, people have found new ways to use natural resources. Thousands of years ago, people learned how to cultivate plants for food, how to use water for irrigation, and how to turn metals into tools. Today, people use natural resources for everything from generating electrical power to sending spacecraft to the stars.

Nonrenewable Resources

Since the Industrial Revolution in the 1800s, when manufacturers in Europe and North America began to use machinery to mass-produce goods in factories, people have been using increasing amounts of Earth's nonrenewable resources. Nonrenewable resources cannot be easily replaced. They exist in fixed amounts or in amounts that are used up more quickly than nature can replace them. It took millions of years for petroleum, natural gas, and coal to form. Yet today, 150 years or so since the Industrial Revolution became widespread, scientists predict that some fossil fuels may run out in a matter of decades.

Mineral resources—which include such diverse materials as metals, gemstones, salt, and rock resources such as sandstone and granite—are also nonrenewable.

▼ Taking care of the soil in a garden requires a lot of hard work. In order for plants to grow well, the soil needs to have the proper amounts of nutrients, air, and water.

Copper and lead are two minerals that may eventually be used up by people.

Even soil is a nonrenewable resource. Fertile soil that is suitable for agriculture forms gradually over thousands of years. Once the nutrients in soil have been depleted, they cannot be easily replaced—and the land is likely to remain barren for generations.

Nuclear power is another nonrenewable resource. It relies on the use of minerals (mainly a type of uranium) that exist in limited amounts.

Renewable Resources

Renewable resources are those that can be easily replaced or that are replenished at rates close to the rates at which they are used. All resources obtained from plants and animals, including wood and food, are renewable. Air, water, wind, and the heat energy from the Sun are other renewable resources. The heat generated in the interior of Earth is a renewable resource called geothermal energy.

Even renewable resources may be threatened. For example, the mismanagement of water resources has caused millions of people around the world to have little or no access to clean, usable freshwater.

Sustainability

Sustainability refers to ways of using natural resources so that the resources are protected while the material needs of people, such as having enough fuel and energy supplies, are also met. In 2002, the United Nations conducted a World Summit on Sustainable Development in Johannesburg, South Africa. Representatives from various nations at the summit pledged to conserve fish populations, end the production of some poisonous chemicals, and work for sustainability in other ways.

Using Natural Resources

Humans and other animals breathe the air (which is also called the atmosphere). The air traps heat near Earth's surface, keeping the planet warm enough to have liquid water and life. And clouds, which produce rain, form in the air.

The cells of all living things need water to carry out numerous biological processes. People use water for drinking, growing food, bathing, cooking, and cleaning. Water is also used to operate factories and to generate electrical power.

People make use of mineral resources to make many products. Metal minerals are important in the construction of houses and skyscrapers and in making automobiles, electronic products, and

even certain medicines. Other mineral resources are used to make concrete, fertilizers, glass, and jewelry.

Soil sustains life by making it possible for people to grow crops. Trees and other plants in nature also depend on fertile soil for their growth, and animals depend on these plants for their survival.

The energy that people use to power everything from cars to computers is generated mainly by fossil fuels. Nuclear power also generates a substantial

▲ People in large cities, such as Shanghai, China, use huge amounts of natural resources. How many different kinds of resources can you identify in this picture? What natural resources were required to erect the buildings and to maintain them?

amount of the energy used in many countries. The renewable energy resources of hydropower (water power), biomass (material from plants and animals), and geothermal, wind, and solar power are expected to meet more of our energy needs in the future.

③ AIR AND WATER

Until recently, people did not worry much about air and water as natural resources. During the twentieth century, however, scientists began to realize that the availability of high-quality air and water was threatened.

Air

The air, or atmosphere, of Earth is a mixture of gases consisting of approximately 78 percent nitrogen, 21 percent oxygen, and 1 percent argon. Smaller amounts of other gases, including carbon dioxide, methane, and water vapor, also occur in the air.

Most of the oxygen in air is produced through photosynthesis. This is the process by which plants use light energy from the Sun to make chemicals called carbohydrates (the plants' food) from carbon dioxide and water. Plants use carbohydrates to grow. During the process of photosynthesis, plants release oxygen into the atmosphere.

Oxygen is used by people and other animals in respiration. In this process oxygen is breathed in and used by the cells of the body to carry out chemical reactions. In the process of respiration, carbon dioxide is released back into the air. This cycling of carbon dioxide is part of Earth's carbon cycle. Carbon dioxide is also released into the air when substances that contain carbon (such as wood or fossil fuels) are burned.

The Greenhouse Effect

Carbon dioxide is a greenhouse gas. Other greenhouse gases in the atmosphere include water vapor, methane, and ozone. These gases act in a similar way to the glass of a greenhouse. They allow heat from the Sun to enter the atmosphere but trap some of the heat radiated by Earth's surface, stopping the heat from escaping. This process is known as the greenhouse effect.

The greenhouse effect makes Earth's surface warm enough to support life. The amount of greenhouse gases in the atmosphere, however, is increasing because of the burning of fossil fuels and other industrial processes. As the level of greenhouse gases increases, more heat is trapped in Earth's atmosphere. Many scientists believe this may be causing global warming, a gradual increase in average temperatures around the world. Scientists are concerned that global warming could lead to rising sea levels caused by melting ice sheets and an increase in extreme weather, such as hurricanes and droughts.

Air Pollution

Smog is a hazy mix of gases and particulates (very small particles). It forms when certain chemicals released by the burning of fossil fuels react with sunlight. Smog may cause or worsen a number of health problems, including asthma and bronchitis. One component of smog is a form of oxygen called ozone. In the lower atmosphere, ozone irritates the eyes and lungs. It also damages plants.

Burning fossil fuels also produces the waste gases sulfur dioxide and nitrogen oxide. These gases react with water vapor in the air to form sulfuric acid and nitric acid. Rain containing high levels of these acids is called acid rain. When acid rain falls, it wears away stone buildings, contaminates soil and water, and damages forests.

▲ Hazy smog over downtown Los Angeles, caused by the burning of fossil fuels in cars and buildings, obscures the city's skyline.

Earth's upper atmosphere contains a layer of ozone gas that blocks most of the Sun's ultraviolet (UV) rays from reaching Earth's surface. The release into the atmosphere of chemicals called chlorofluorocarbons (CFCs) has made a region in the ozone layer thinner. The region where the ozone layer is thinner is known as the ozone hole. CFCs, made of chlorine, fluorine, and carbon, were formerly used in large amounts to make aerosol sprays, plastic foams, and the refrigerants in refrigerators, freezers, and air conditioners. The ozone hole allows a greater-than-normal amount of UV rays to reach Earth's surface. These rays can cause skin cancer and other health problems in people and other animals.

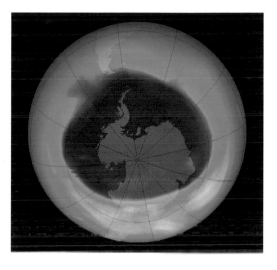

▲ A colored image made by a satellite shows the ozone hole (blue), a region over Antarctica in which the atmosphere's protective ozone layer becomes less concentrated every spring. Temperature changes at that time cause ozone-destroying chemical reactions between CFCs and ozone.

Reducing Air Pollution

Much progress has been made since the 1970s in reducing air pollution and addressing related concerns. Because of warnings from scientists about the possible harmful effects of global warming, many governments and industries have acted to reduce emissions of carbon dioxide and other greenhouse gases. The Kyoto Protocol, signed by most of the world's countries, requires industrialized nations to decrease the rate at which greenhouse gases enter the atmosphere.

Smog and other forms of air pollution have been reduced since the Clean Air Act was passed by the U.S. Congress in 1970. This act required automobiles to have devices called catalytic converters, which are fitted to exhaust systems to reduce emissions from engines. The act also made it compulsory for power plants and factories to use systems known as smokestack scrubbers. These systems reduce emissions of sulfur dioxide and other pollutants. Government statistics indicate that since the act was passed, dust particle emissions have

Dinosaur Breath

The average person takes about 23,000 breaths each day. Every time you breathe, you take millions of oxygen molecules into your lungs. These are the same oxygen molecules that have been circulating around Earth for millions of years. They are continuously reused and recycled. In fact, some of the oxygen molecules inside your lungs now may be the same molecules that were once in the lungs of a *Tyrannosaurus rex*!

been reduced in the United States by 75 percent, sulfur dioxide emissions by 35 percent, and carbon monoxide and ozone by 30 percent.

The United States has not produced CFCs since 1996, and these chemicals are no longer produced in most other countries. Scientists expect the ozone layer to eventually recover.

Water

Water makes up two-thirds of your body. It is needed for all biological processes. Water covers more than 70 percent of Earth's surface. Almost all of this water— 97 percent—is salt water in the oceans and seas. Only 3 percent is freshwater. Two-thirds of this freshwater is locked up as ice in glaciers and in the ice caps at the North and South Poles. The remaining 1 percent of freshwater is in rivers and lakes, aquifers (underground water reservoirs), and the atmosphere.

From the world's relatively small amount of freshwater, people satisfy

virtually all their water needs, including drinking, bathing, growing crops, cooking, cleaning, and carrying away wastes. They also use freshwater for many industrial purposes. In addition, the falling freshwater of river dams and waterfalls serves as a resource to generate electricity.

▲ An irrigation system sprays large amounts of water over a field of growing potato plants.

Worries About Water

Water is continuously recycled in Earth's water cycle, or hydrologic cycle. Almost all rainwater that falls to the planet's surface flows to the ocean in rivers or underground streams. Once in the ocean, the water is warmed by the Sun and evaporates back into the atmosphere. In the atmosphere, the water vapor condenses into water droplets, which form clouds. The water then falls back to the ground as rain or other precipitation.

Unfortunately, the quality of the water in this great cycle can be damaged to the point where the water is unusable. Human and animal wastes, toxic (poisonous) industrial chemicals, and harmful pesticides and fertilizers pollute rivers, lakes, and groundwater supplies, as well as parts of the ocean. This pollution makes the water unhealthy to consume, and it kills fish and other organisms that live in the water.

Furthermore, the quantity of usable, drinkable water is declining in some parts of the world. For example, groundwater is being used up in the southwestern United States and other arid regions. As the water in the ground is used up, the water table (the upper limit of an underground water supply) becomes lower and lower. It then costs more money to pump the water from the ground. In addition, water from lower levels usually contains more contaminants than upper-level water does.

In Las Vegas, Nevada, a city built in the desert, the water table has declined as much as 300 feet (91.4 meters) since the early 1900s as the population of the city has exploded. The lowering water table has caused the earth above it to shift, which has led to a sinking of the land by as much as 6 feet (2 m) in places.

▲ The bustling city of Las Vegas spreads across the Nevada desert. The massive use of groundwater by the city has led to a lowering of the water table and, in turn, a shifting and sinking of the land.

In parts of the world, an even bigger problem is the frequent occurrence of droughts. Long periods without rain have resulted in shortages of fresh water, leading to millions of deaths in Africa in recent years. Lack of investment by

Using Water from the Sea

Salt can be removed from seawater in a process called desalination. When the salt has been removed, the water can be used for drinking, agriculture, and other purposes. Water from desalination facilities is used by many military posts, oil-drilling crews, and island resorts that have limited supplies of freshwater. Major U.S. desalination facilities include those at Naval Station Guantanamo Bay, Cuba, and at resort areas in Cape Coral and Sanibel Island, Florida.

African governments in water storage facilities, treatment plants, and distribution systems has contributed to this water shortage problem.

Protecting Water Resources

In the United States, water pollution is less of a problem today than it was during the mid- to late-twentieth century. Two landmark U.S. antipollution laws were the Clean Water Act of 1971 and the Safe Drinking Water Act of 1974.

The Clean Water Act gave the U.S. Environmental Protection Agency (EPA) the power to establish regulations to reduce the amount of pollutants being discharged into waterways. The Safe Drinking Water Act authorized the EPA to set standards to reduce harmful bacteria, chemicals, and metallic compounds in public water systems. Many rivers and lakes now have fewer pollutants than they once did, and the populations of many species of fish have recovered.

Experts from the United Nations and from the United States and other countries are working with authorities in Africa and elsewhere to find better ways of managing their water resources.

Typical Indoor Water Use in U.S. Households

This table represents the relative amounts of water that are used indoors in a typical U.S. household. Outdoor water use varies greatly across the United States. For example, outdoor water use represents 7 percent of all household water use in Pennsylvania but 70 percent in the Las Vegas area of Nevada.

Indoor Use	% Water Use
Toilets	41%
Showers/Baths	33%
Clothes Washers/ Other Cleaning	21%
Kitchen	5%

4 MINERAL RESOURCES

Earth's crust (outer rocky layer) is like a giant storehouse of some three thousand kinds of minerals. The word *mineral* is commonly used to identify any nonliving substance taken from the ground, including fossil fuels and rocks. Mineralogists, however, consider true minerals to be made of substances that were never alive (unlike fossil fuels) and substances that have the same chemical makeup no matter where they are found (unlike many kinds of rocks).

Metals

Metals are typically shiny materials that conduct electricity and heat. People use metals to make electrical items, such as power cords, and electronic products, such as the parts inside computers. Metals are also used to make buildings, batteries, jewelry, and medicines.

Ores are minerals that contain enough metals to make them worth mining. Some ores occur in Earth's crust as native metals, which are pure metals. Copper, gold, platinum, and

▲ Mineral resources include metals, such as gold *(top left)*; rock-forming substances, such as feldspar *(top right)* and quartz *(bottom left)*; and sulfur *(bottom right)*, which is in iron ore, coal, and other substances.

silver are usually found as native metals. Other ores occur in Earth's crust as compound ores. These are metals that are joined to other substances. Metals that occur naturally as compound ores include aluminum, iron, lead, and tin. Metals are separated from ores in various ways, including crushing and grinding, melting, and exposing them to electric currents.

Aluminum

Aluminum is the most plentiful metal in Earth's crust, making up about 8 percent of the planet's outer layer. It occurs naturally in deposits of bauxite, an ore that also contains other minerals and water. Most bauxite occurs in tropical or subtropical regions of the world.

Because aluminum is lightweight, it can be formed into almost any shape. It can be used as thin foil to wrap chewing gum or, if rolled together into thick plates, as armor for tanks. Aluminum cans are the world's most commonly recycled drink containers.

▲ Because of aluminum's flexibility, it can be formed into a wide variety of products, including rims for automobile wheels.

Copper

Copper is a reddish-orange metal that is rather scarce in Earth's crust. It is one of the most useful metals. It can be made into electronic products, house gutters, jewelry, pennies, plumbing fixtures, pots, doorknobs, and many other items. Because it conducts electricity well, copper is also made into electrical wire for telephone and television systems.

▲ Copper wire is the most commonly used metal wire for conducting electricity. Although silver is a better conductor, its expense prevents it from being widely used in electrical wire.

Copper is easily formed into alloys (mixtures of metals). Brass is an alloy of copper and zinc, while bronze is an alloy of mostly copper and tin. Copper can be easily recycled from scrap wire, electrical equipment, automobile radiators, and other products.

Iron

Iron is a common metal in Earth's crust, usually found combined with various other substances. In the presence of water, iron combines easily with oxygen, forming iron oxide (also known as rust).

Iron is used as a raw material to make everything from paper clips to skyscrapers. Manufacturers obtain metallic iron from iron ores by crushing the ores and melting the resulting iron concentrates in furnaces. Steelmakers continue heating the liquid iron, often with recycled iron and steel scrap, in furnaces to refine (purify) it. The addition of a small amount of carbon to the purified iron converts the iron into steel.

▼ The Golden Gate Bridge, which spans the entrance to San Francisco Bay, is made of 83,000 tons (75,000 metric tons) of steel, 390,000 cubic yards (300,000 cubic meters) of concrete, and 160,000 miles (260,000 kilometers) of wire.

Fool's Gold

People have always prized gold for its beauty and rarity. A type of iron ore, however, has fooled many people. This type of iron ore looks like gold. Pyrite, or "fool's gold," is an ore made of iron and sulfur. It is found in many places around the world. When people see its yellowish color, they may mistakenly think they have found gold.

Precious Metals

People value certain metals beyond all other metals. These precious metals—which are difficult to find or expensive to mine and process—include gold, silver, and platinum.

Gold

Gold has been the most sought-after metal in the world for thousands of years. People value it not only for its luster and beauty but also because it is very malleable (easy to shape)—which makes it extremely useful. For thousands of years, people have used it to make coins and jewelry. Today, because it is an excellent conductor of electricity and heat, gold is also used in computers and other electronic devices, and as thermal insulation on spacecraft to reflect the infrared (heat) rays of the Sun.

Gold in History

Gold jewelry dates back to at least 4000 B.C., the approximate date of jewelry uncovered in Varna, Bulgaria, which is on the coast of the Black Sea. The earliest gold coins are from Lydia (modern western Turkey), dating from the 500s B.C. Today, gold jewelry and coins remain very valuable. The United States, however, has not minted gold coins as legal currency since 1933, when the U.S. government stopped basing the value of its money on gold.

Silver

Archaeologists have unearthed silver ornaments and coins that are more than six thousand years old. Today, people use silver to make not only jewelry and money but also tableware, photographic film, electrical wire, amalgam dental fillings, and pharmaceuticals. Because silver helps kill bacteria, some drainage tubes and other instruments used in surgical procedures are made from silver.

Silver is a very soft metal, so manufacturers usually add copper to it to increase its hardness and usefulness. Sterling silver is an alloy of 92.5 percent silver and 7.5 percent copper.

Platinum

The silvery-white metal called platinum is even more valuable than gold. Platinum is malleable, it does not rust or tarnish, and it resists melting at extreme temperatures. Platinum is used for many purposes, including making electrical equipment, surgical instruments, laboratory catalysts (substances that speed up chemical reactions), and jewelry. Catalytic converters are made with platinum because the platinum helps break down harmful nitrogen oxides in vehicle exhaust.

Nonmetals

Earth's mineral resources include a wide variety of nonmetallic minerals. Some of these minerals are probably very familiar to you. Others may not be as well known, but they are still important.

Salt

The salt you may sprinkle on your food is a chemical compound named sodium chloride. This compound comes from a mineral called rock salt (also known as halite). Rock salt deposits, which are found underground on every continent, formed millions of years ago when sea-water evaporated, leaving the salt behind. In some places, such as along the Gulf Coast of North America, deposits of rock salt occur above ground as salt domes.

Because rock salt lowers the melting point of ice, it is commonly spread on streets in winter to melt ice. Chlorine comes from rock salt. It is used to make cleaning fluids, paper, plastics, and pesticides.

▲ At the Janubio saltworks on the island of Lanzarote, in the Canary Islands of Spain, mounds of salt accumulate as trapped seawater evaporates in the Sun.

Chemicals in the Crust

Oxygen is the most abundant element in Earth's crust, making up 47 percent of the weight of the rocks in the crust. The second most abundant element is silicon, making up 27 percent. These elements usually occur in combination as silica, making up three-fourths of Earth's crust. The next most common elements are aluminum (8 percent), iron (5 percent), calcium (4 percent), and sodium, potassium, and magnesium (about 2 percent each).

Silica

Silica is a chemical compound of silicon and oxygen. Silicates, such as feldspars and micas, are various kinds of rock-forming minerals containing silica. Silica is an important material that is used in the manufacture of various products, including ceramics, cosmetics, glass, insulation, paints, paper, pharmaceuticals, plastics, and steel.

Gypsum

Have you ever made a plaster of Paris statue or had to wear a plaster cast on a broken arm or leg? If so, then you are familiar with gypsum, a yellowish-white mineral made of calcium and sulfate. Gypsum is used to make plaster of Paris powder, which in turn is used for craft projects and some surgical casts. Gypsum is also used in the construction industry to make plasterboard and wallboard.

Phosphates

Phosphates, which are made of phosphorus and oxygen atoms, are among the most important molecules in your body. Together with calcium, phosphates give strength to your bones. Phosphates also form parts of DNA (the molecule that makes up genes) and RNA (a molecule that helps produce proteins). The phosphates found in nature are used to make fertilizers and other products.

Gemstones

Some of the most valuable minerals in the world are gemstones—minerals such as diamonds, emeralds, opals, and rubies. People value gemstones mainly for their colors, brilliance, and rarity and use them to make jewelry and ornaments. Some gemstones, such as diamonds, also have a number of uses in industry. Because diamonds are so hard, they make excellent grinding, cutting, and boring tools. Gemstones occur naturally throughout the world in many kinds of rocks.

▲ Diamonds, which are the hardest naturally occurring substance on Earth, can be cut and polished so that they reflect and bend rays of light.

Rock Resources

Metallic and nonmetallic minerals are very important to everyday life, but there are other, related natural resources that are even more widely used. These are the rock resources, such as sandstone, limestone, granite, and marble. These rock resources are crucial to construction projects throughout the world.

Sandstone and Limestone

Many historic buildings in towns and cities across North America, as well as many great cathedrals and other structures in Europe and elsewhere, are built from sandstone or limestone. Sandstone is a type of rock made mostly of sand that has been cemented together by pressure and minerals. Depending on its exact composition, sandstone may be cream-colored, gray, red, brown, or green. Limestone consists of calcium carbonate (lime). Some limestone is formed from the broken-up shells or other remains of such marine organisms as corals, clams, snails, and sea urchins. Other limestone is made from lime deposits that were once at the bottom of oceans.

Granite

Granite is a hard, durable rock that is useful for constructing buildings. It is

Chicago Water Tower

The Chicago Water Tower, which was completed in 1869, was one of the few structures to survive the Great Chicago Fire of 1871. The tower, designed by architect William W. Boyington, was constructed of limestone blocks quarried in nearby Joliet, Illinois. The Water Tower remains a major tourist attraction in downtown Chicago. Contrary to popular belief, however, it was not the only structure to survive the Great Chicago Fire.

▲ The Chicago Water Tower is one of many structures built in the 1800s of limestone quarried in Joliet.

so hard and strong because it is made of minerals (including quartz and feldspar) that are locked tightly together like pieces of a jigsaw puzzle. Granite can withstand the effects of weathering for centuries. Because it is so long-lasting, people have often used it to build historic monuments and sculptures.

Marble

Marble is another long-lasting rock that is widely used to construct buildings and monuments. Most marble is made from limestone that was exposed to intense heat and pressure in Earth's crust. These forces caused changes in the texture and makeup of the limestone, leading to the formation of various kinds of mineral impurities. The particular impurities that occur in marble give it a wide variety of patterns and colors, including white, red, yellow, and green.

Mining Minerals

Mineral deposits at Earth's surface are the source of some minerals. Other minerals are mined from far beneath the ground.

Two examples of surface mining are placer mining and open-pit mining. In placer mining, miners use water to remove gold, platinum, tin, and other metals from gravel and sand. They shovel gravel and sand into a slanting wooden trough and wash them with water. The water flow causes the heavy minerals to settle in grooves at the bottom of the trough. In open-pit mining, miners first remove the layer of rock lying over an

▲ In this photograph of an open-pit copper mine you can see where miners have removed layers of surface rock to expose subsurface ore deposits.

What Do Mining Engineers Do?

Mining engineers plan and direct all engineering aspects of mining operations. They conduct investigations of mineral deposits and work with geologists and economists to determine the best mining methods to use in different cases. A person interested in becoming a mining engineer should learn about chemistry, physics, math, and problem solving.

ore deposit. They then use explosives to break up the ore-bearing rock, and mine the exposed layers of ore.

In underground mining, miners first dig an opening into the mine. A vertical opening is called a shaft, and a horizontal opening (in the side of a mountain) is called an adit. As miners move through the passage, they must support the walls of the opening with waste material from the excavation or with posts and beams.

How Long Will Minerals Last?

Geological exploration of Earth's crust has revealed that the reserves of some minerals are relatively small, while the reserves of other minerals are enormous. The proved (or known) reserves of copper, lead, nickel, and zinc may be depleted within a hundred years. However, the proved reserves of aluminum, iron, and certain other minerals are so vast that they are likely to last several hundred more years.

Although some minerals exist in vast quantities, people will have to keep exploring farther and digging deeper to obtain these minerals in the future. The extra effort and expense involved in this extraction is likely to add to the costs of these minerals.

To help conserve Earth's mineral resources, some items that are made from minerals, such as copper pipes, can be recycled. There are also synthetic substitutes for some minerals, such as imitation gemstones.

Deep Ocean Mining

Earth's mineral resources might last longer than expected if new mining techniques can be developed. For example, new techniques may make it less expensive to mine minerals from the deep ocean floor. In 2006, geologists were investigating the use of robotic mining machines to extract valuable minerals at depths of more than 1.2 miles (2 km) below the sea's surface.

5 SOIL RESOURCES

Soil is a very important natural resource that is often overlooked. Plants get the nutrients they need from soil, and animals get their nutrients from plants or from animals that eat plants. Without high-quality soil, neither farms nor forests could thrive.

What Is Soil?

Soil is a lot more than just dirt! It contains many different minerals and nutrients and decaying plant and animal matter (which releases more nutrients into the soil). A wide variety of organisms (including bacteria, fungi, earthworms, and insects) live in the soil. These organisms find the water and air they need in spaces between soil particles.

Different areas contain different kinds of soil. Some soils are yellow or red, while others are dark brown or black. The color of soil is an indication of the amounts of minerals, decaying matter, water, and air it contains. Some soils have large mineral particles, and others have small particles. Sands have the largest particles, which can be easily seen and felt. Silts also have large particles that can be seen. Clays have particles that are microscopic in size. Water drains through the large, loose particles of sand more easily than through the tiny, tight particles of clay.

▲ Sandy soil *(left)* has a rough texture, while clays *(right)* have a smooth, sticky texture. Loamy soil *(center)*, made of a combination of sand, silt, and clay, is not as smooth or sticky as clays.

How Soil Forms

Soil begins to form when the effects of wind, water, freezing, thawing, and other environmental conditions break down rocks into mineral particles. This process is called weathering. When plants and animals die, they add nutritious organic material to the soil.

Over time, different layers—called horizons—typically develop in soil. The surface layer of leaf litter and other organic debris that decomposes into the soil is the O horizon. This horizon merges into the topsoil—the A horizon. The next layer the B horizon—contains minerals washed down from the surface. The C horizon contains rocks and other material and is just above the bedrock, the solid layer of rock beneath the soil.

Topsoil contains large amounts of nutrient-rich humus, a dark brown substance that forms when bacteria, fungi, and other decomposers break down dead plant and animal material. Topsoil is usually 4 to 10 inches (10 to 25 centimeters) deep—deep enough to support plant roots. Rich, nutritious topsoil can take hundreds of years to develop.

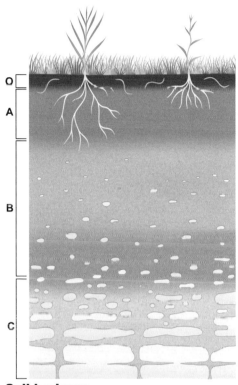

Soil horizons

▲ The four main layers of soil consist of *(from top to bottom)* leaf litter and other organic debris (O horizon), topsoil (A horizon), minerals washed down from the surface (B horizon), and rocks and other material lying above the bedrock (C horizon).

Nutrient Cycles

Nitrogen and phosphorus are two nutrients that continuously circulate in cycles among soil, plants, animals, and other parts of the environment. There are many parts to these cycles. In one part, bacteria in the soil convert (or *fix*) nitrogen from the atmosphere into chemical substances that plants can use for growth. Fixed nitrogen may be circulated many times among plants, animals, and the soil before other bacteria in the soil convert it back into gaseous compounds that return to the atmosphere.

Soil's Master Gardeners

Earthworms are important in helping to maintain the fertility of soil. As these "master gardeners" burrow their way through the soil—eating plant material and leaving wastes behind—they help add organic matter to the soil's humus. Worms also loosen the soil particles, allowing air and water to mix throughout the ground.

▲ Soil would not stay fertile without the "gardening" help of small invertebrates such as earthworms.

Soil Erosion and Degradation

What took hundreds of years to form can be wiped out in the virtual blink of an eye. Unwise farming and forestry practices damage and destroy topsoil every day, as do various kinds of chemical pollutants and other factors. When soil is degraded or damaged, it becomes less productive and less able to support plant and animal life.

Erosion is a natural process in which rock and soil break down and move from one place to another. This normally happens in a gradual way that does little harm to soil. However, a number of human activities increase soil erosion. For example, when people remove plants with large root systems from an area, the roots no longer hold the topsoil in place. Heavy rains may then wash away the topsoil. Erosion often washes valuable nutrients out of farmland.

Soil can be degraded in other ways, too. For example, it can become contaminated by salt or toxic chemicals, and grazing livestock may remove its plant cover. Excessive irrigation can make soil waterlogged and lead to a rise in the water table. As the groundwater approaches the surface, it evaporates, leaving behind salt that was in the irrigation water. Over time, this salt builds up in the soil, eventually reaching levels that are harmful to plants. According to some estimates, approximately 65,000 acres (26,000 hectares) of the world's topsoil are lost to salt buildup every day.

Soil erosion and degradation are growing problems throughout the world—

Soil Erosion in Ancient Greece

Soil erosion and degradation are not a new problem. The philosopher Plato (427–347 B.C.) made the following observations about soil erosion in ancient Greece: "Attica yielded far more abundant produce. In comparison of what then was there are remaining only the bones of the wasted body; all the richer and softer parts of the soil having fallen away, and the mere skeleton of the land being left."

▼ A researcher examines the degraded soil in California's San Joaquin Valley. The land here has a number of problems, including contamination with toxic chemicals and sinking caused by groundwater depletion.

including in the United States. In the San Joaquin Valley of California, high levels of the chemical element selenium (from oil refinery wastewater) have contaminated farmland, groundwater, and a wildlife refuge.

Desertification

Soil erosion and degradation can lead to desertification, causing land that was once fertile and productive to become infertile, unproductive, and barren. Millions of acres of cultivated land, in arid and semi-arid regions of the world, are lost to desertification every year. The Food and Agriculture Organization of the United Nations estimates that more than 250 million people are directly affected by the loss of soil because of desertification, and some 1 billion others are at risk of being affected by this problem.

▲ Decades of drought and soil erosion caused by livestock overgrazing have led to increased desertification in the Sahel, a region south of the Sahara in Africa.

Soil Conservation

As people have become more aware of the importance of preserving topsoil, they have developed effective ways to conserve this important and previously overlooked resource.

Farmers can slow the erosion of topsoil by planting trees and by leaving natural plants in unplowed areas. The trees serve as windbreaks, helping to prevent the wind from eroding the soil. The plant cover reduces runoff from rainwater. Some farmers use a method called strip cropping to protect the soil from erosion. In this method, farmers plant grass, clover, or other low-growing plants between rows of other crops. The low-growing plants protect the soil, and bacteria in clover roots fix nitrogen in the soil.

Many farmers use a method called contour plowing on sloping land to reduce erosion. In this method, farmers plow the soil across the slope, and the plowed soil forms ridges that help slow the flow of rainwater. Terracing is another method that can help reduce soil erosion on hillsides. Farmers construct wide, flat rows called terraces on the hillsides—they look a bit like huge stairs. The terraces hold rainwater, preventing it from washing down the hill.

What Is an Agronomist?

Agronomists are scientists who study ways to make soils more productive. They carefully examine soils, testing them for chemical substances important for plant growth. They also seek new ways to conserve soils, reduce soil erosion, and solve problems related to soil and water pollution. Agronomists may work for private companies, universities, or government agencies.

Many farmers use crop rotation to prevent soil degradation. In this method, they alternate crops from year to year. They may plant corn or wheat one year and alfalfa or soybeans the next year. Bacteria in the roots of the alfalfa and soybeans fix nitrogen in the soil.

Managers of forests can protect soil from erosion by leaving dead branches, leaves, and other material on the forest floor. When this material decays, it adds to the organic content of the soil. In addition, forestry managers preserve large groupings of trees because the roots of the trees help hold the soil in place.

Soil-Saving Spectroscopy

A technology called infrared spectroscopy is being used to help analyze degraded soils in Africa. With this technology, light is shone onto a soil sample, and the amount of light reflected by the sample at different wavelengths is detected and measured. The specific wavelengths detected provide information about the soil's chemical properties, which, in turn, help scientists better evaluate the degree of degradation and other problems in the soil.

▼ Rice is grown on terraced hillsides in China. The terraces hold water and reduce soil erosion.

6 FOSSIL FUEL RESOURCES

We use large amounts of natural resources for energy to power machines, fuel vehicles, and heat, cool, and light buildings. In most cases, the energy we use is generated by the combustion (burning) of fossil fuels—coal, petroleum (crude oil), and natural gas. Fossil fuels consist mainly of a mixture of molecules called hydrocarbons, which are chemical compounds containing hydrogen and carbon.

▲ An oil pump jack (the aboveground drive for an underground pump) towers over the prairie in Alberta, Canada.

Petroleum includes both crude oil and natural gas (although in common usage and in this book, *petroleum* refers mainly to crude oil). Crude oil is used for approximately 40 percent of the commercial energy (energy produced by businesses and governments and sold to the public) in the United States and the rest of the world. Natural gas and coal each supply roughly 23 percent of the commercial energy used in the United States and the rest of the world.

Formation of Fossil Fuels

Fossil fuels get their name from the fact that they developed over millions of years from the fossilized remains of dead plants, animals, and other organisms. Petroleum (including both oil and gas) formed from tiny plantlike organisms called algae and tiny animals called zooplankton that lived in the water along coastlines hundreds of millions of years ago. As these organisms died, their remains settled on the seafloor and were buried in sediment (sand, mud, and

Carboniferous Coal Swamp

Coal formed in swamps mainly during the Carboniferous Period, from about 359 million to 299 million years ago. Fossilized remains of large plants and animals are sometimes found in coal beds. These fossils show that several types of trees related to modern ferns grew in the swamps. Animals in these prehistoric swamps included giant dragonflies as well as amphibians the size of crocodiles.

▶ A fossil shows the leaves of a seed fern, a type of tree that grew in swamps 300 million years ago. Much of the coal we use today formed from the remains of seed ferns.

other material). Over time, the remains and sediment built up, and the pressure and temperature inside the mix increased. The pressure compressed the sediment into rock, and the heat and chemical reactions converted the organic remains into crude oil and natural gas.

Coal formed in swampy areas from dead trees and other plants. The constantly wet conditions slowed the normal process in which bacteria cause the decomposition of organic material. So the plant material changed into a partially decayed substance called peat. As the peat became buried in sediment at the bottom of the swamps, its pressure and temperature increased. These conditions caused the carbon and hydrogen in the material to squeeze together more tightly, forcing out the water and gases. As the carbon increased in concentration, the peat gradually turned into coal with various ranks of carbon content.

Petroleum

Petroleum companies process different mixtures of hydrocarbons in petroleum to make substances with different uses, such as transportation fuels, heating oil, and lubricants.

Gasoline is the most common transportation fuel made from petroleum. Other petroleum fuels include diesel fuel (used by trains, ships, buses, and large trucks), jet fuel, and various fuels used to heat buildings.

Manufacturers use petrochemicals, chemical compounds obtained from petroleum, as raw materials to make hundreds of products. These products include plastics, synthetic fibers (such as polyester), cosmetics, detergents, fertilizers, pesticides, and pharmaceuticals.

The United States and most other industrialized nations use far more petroleum than they can produce themselves, so they have to import petroleum from other countries. In 2004 (the last year for

Middle East Oil

Some of the countries that the United States depends on for petroleum are in the politically unstable, conflict-ridden Middle East. This dependence has led to many problems. In the 1970s, the Organization of Petroleum Exporting Countries (OPEC), an association of mostly Arab nations that produce and export petroleum, stopped shipping petroleum to the United States to protest U.S. support of Israel in Israel's conflict with Syria and Egypt. This oil embargo resulted in a severe gasoline shortage, high gasoline prices, and long lines of cars at gas stations throughout the United States.

which data was available at the time of this book's publication), the United States produced a total of 5,430,000

Plastics from Petroleum

Look around your home and you are sure to find many items made of plastic. Many people do not realize that most plastic—just like gasoline and oil—comes from petroleum. Plastic is made from substances called synthetic resins, which are produced from carbon- and hydrogen-containing molecules found in crude oil, natural gas, and coal.

▶ Most plastic bottles and other plastic products are made from chemicals obtained from petroleum.

barrels of crude oil every day. In the same year, the United States imported almost 13 million barrels of oil every day from other countries.

Natural Gas

Natural gas is different from gasoline. Gasoline is a liquid fuel that is made from crude oil. Natural gas is a gaseous substance, like air or steam. It is a fossil fuel that is often found on top of deposits of crude oil.

Natural gas consists mostly of a type of hydrocarbon called methane. In homes, natural gas is used for heating, cooling, cooking, burning garbage, drying laundry, and other purposes. In industry, natural gas heat is used to manufacture products such as glass, paper, steel, and textiles. Natural gas is also used to generate electric power and operate farm equipment, and as a fuel for some vehicles. Many petrochemicals are derived from natural gas.

Natural gas liquids are liquid fuels that are made from natural gas. These include ethane, propane, and butane. Natural gas liquids have many different uses. If you have ever eaten food cooked on an outdoor gas grill that uses propane, you have enjoyed a common use of natural gas liquids.

▲ Many people are most familiar with natural gas as the blue flames used to cook food on gas stoves.

Some natural gas is found in the frozen ground of the Arctic as gas hydrates, which are solids that look like wet snow. Natural gas can also be extracted from coal.

The United States produced 18,776 billion cubic feet (532 billion cu m) of natural gas in 2004. It imported 4,259 billion cubic feet (121 billion cu m) of natural gas in the same year to meet its consumption needs.

Coal

The energy industry uses coal to produce high-pressure steam in boilers, which in turn is used to generate electric power. Coal is also used as a raw material to make steel, cement, dyes, fertilizer, and many other products. Most roads are paved with asphalt and other material derived from the processing of coal.

Coal consists mainly of carbon, hydrogen, nitrogen, oxygen, and sulfur. Sulfur limits the usefulness of coal because it combines with oxygen to form the gas sulfur dioxide, which is a major cause of air pollution. Most coal-burning power plants in the United States use scrubbers, which reduce sulfur dioxide emissions.

Approximately 60 percent of the coal mined in the world comes from surface mines. Most of this coal is obtained through a method called strip mining.

In strip mining, miners remove strips of land to expose the coal deposits on the sides of hills or mountains. Other coal comes from underground mines.

The world uses more than 5 billion tons (4.5 billion MT) of coal every year, with the United States using some 20 percent of this total.

Coal Miners

Despite improvements in safety in the past hundred years, coal mining remains a dangerous profession. Serious accidents happen, such as when mine roof supports fail and mines collapse. Mine hazards also come from methane, an explosive gas, and carbon monoxide, a poisonous gas. Breathing in large amounts of coal dust can lead to a fatal respiratory disease called pneumoconiosis, also called black lung.

▼ Rescue workers assist one of 33 coal miners who were trapped in a flooded mine shaft in Russia in October 2003. All but two of the miners in this accident were brought to the surface alive.

The United States produced 1,111 million tons (1,008 million MT) of coal in 2004, while using 1,104 million tons (1,002 million MT) for its own consumption.

Environmental Problems Caused by Fossil Fuels

Many of the problems caused by the combustion of fossil fuels are addressed in Chapter 2, the chapter on air and water. These problems include smog and acid rain, as well as an increase in levels of greenhouse gases, such as carbon dioxide, in Earth's atmosphere.

Coal generates the most air pollutants of any fossil fuel, while natural gas generates the fewest. Coal used to be widely used to heat homes in the United States. Many older people remember the days

Cleaning Up Oil Spills

When crude oil accidentally spills from tankers at sea, millions of gallons may flow into the water and onto beaches. The oil coats fish, birds, and mammals, causing the deaths of many animals. Emergency workers can clean up some of the oil in spills. In a method called biodegradation, workers add certain kinds of bacteria or other microbes to the spill. These microbes break down the harmful chemical compounds in the oil into harmless substances. However, much of the oil in a spill moves to different locations, drifting and dispersing in the sea or sinking to the bottom.

▼ Most of the energy used to light large cities such as Chicago comes from power stations that burn fossil fuels to generate electricity.

when air pollution caused by the burning of coal was so bad that it turned the snow black! That sometimes happened before the government passed antipollution laws and before people began to use natural gas more widely as a cleaner substitute for coal.

Fossil fuels are also the culprit in oil spills, the leaking of crude oil into the environment. Oil occasionally leaks from wells, pipelines, and tankers. Sometimes, individuals who use oil for their own needs spill it into the environment. Oil spills can contaminate water supplies, kill plants and animals, and be very difficult to clean up.

How Long Will Fossil Fuels Last?

Experts predict that different fossil fuels will last for different lengths of time. The length of time that supplies will last is not only related to the amounts of fossil fuels in the ground. It is also related to changes in the rates at which people use the different fossil fuels and in the ability to extract these fuels. Advances in mining technology may make it easier to extract some supplies that are currently out of reach.

Experts in the petroleum industry believe that crude oil and natural gas supplies will last until at least 2050.

Petroleum supplies might last for a hundred years or longer if new techniques can be developed to make it easier to obtain natural gas from gas hydrates in the frozen ground of the Arctic. Supplies might also last longer if more natural gas can be extracted from coal. Experts believe that enough coal exists to last more than a thousand years.

Petroleum Consumption in Various Countries (2003)

Country	Amount Used (Millions of Barrels Per Day)
Brazil	2.10
Canada	2.19
China	5.55
France	2.06
India	2.32
Japan	5.58
Mexico	2.02
Russia	2.68
United Kingdom	1.72
United States	20.03
World Total	80.10

NUCLEAR AND RENEWABLE ENERGY

The world's demand for energy is likely to keep increasing—in both industrialized countries (which use the most energy) and developing countries (which will use more energy as they become more industrialized). To meet these growing needs, the world is moving beyond fossil fuels to use increasing amounts of other forms of energy— nuclear power and various forms of renewable energy resources, including hydropower, biomass, and geothermal, wind, and solar power.

Nuclear Power

The energy that produces the heat and light of the Sun is nuclear energy, which results from changes or reactions in the nuclei (cores) of atoms. We can harness nuclear energy, using controlled nuclear reactions, to create power in nuclear power plants. Nuclear energy is also released in the massive violent explosions of nuclear weapons.

Most nuclear reactors in electric power plants use the radioactive metal uranium as a raw material. Inside the reactor, very

▲ Many nuclear power plants, such as this one in Germany, have large cooling towers (foreground) that release steam produced from hot water surrounding the nuclear reactor vessels in the plants.

tiny particles bombard atoms of uranium. This causes the fission (splitting) of the nuclei in the uranium atoms. As the nuclei split, vast amounts of energy are released. The fission of 1 pound (0.45 kilogram) of uranium releases more energy than the burning of 3 million pounds (1.4 million kg) of coal.

Unlike power plants that burn fossil fuels, nuclear power plants release no greenhouse gases or smog into the air. However, nuclear power plants produce large amounts of radioactive wastes that can remain harmful for thousands of years. Exposure to this radioactive material could cause cancer and many other health problems.

The United States produced and used 8.23 quadrillion British thermal units (Btu) of nuclear electric power in 2004. This use represented approximately 8 percent of the total U.S. energy consumption that year.

Hydropower

Hydropower is the use of moving water to generate energy. The power of moving water can be converted into electrical energy in hydroelectric power plants and—to a much lesser extent—in tidal power stations.

Most hydroelectric power plants are built on rivers. These facilities store river water in a reservoir behind a dam. To generate power, this water is released to fall to a turbine at a lower level. The rushing water causes the turbine shaft to rotate, driving an electric generator.

Hydroelectric power plants use a renewable resource and do not release air pollutants. Their use, however, is possible only in places where there are large rivers. Furthermore, some environmentalists oppose hydroelectric facilities because they believe the dams harm river habitats. The United States obtained

The Chernobyl Incident

A small number of accidents have occurred at nuclear power plants in the past fifty years. The most serious accident happened at the Chernobyl nuclear reactor in the Ukraine (part of the former Soviet Union) in April 1986. A flawed design in the reactor led to an explosion and fire that released radioactive material into the atmosphere. Winds carried the material over the Ukraine, Russia, and other parts of Europe. As of 2006, more than fifty deaths from cancer and other problems related to the Chernobyl incident had been reported. Some experts believe, however, that many more people will die from cancer caused by the incident.

about 3 percent of its energy from hydro-electric power plants in 2004.

Tidal power stations are based on harnessing the energy of tides, the periodic rising and falling of water in the ocean and large lakes. Dams at tidal power stations store water when the tide is high and then release it to turn turbines as the tide falls. There are only a few tidal power stations in the world, the largest of which is located on the Rance River in northern France.

▼ The falling water at Wanapum Dam, on the Columbia River in Washington State, has been generating electricity since the 1960s.

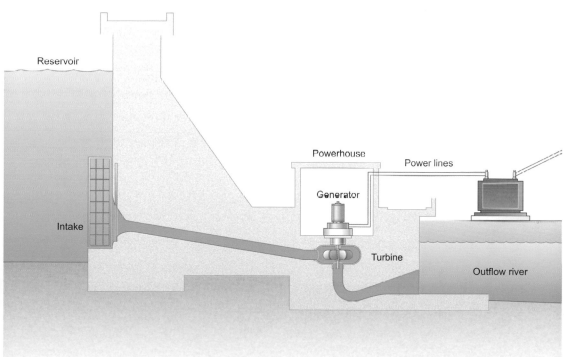

▲ In a typical hydroelectric power plant, water is stored in a reservoir behind a dam. When the water is released, it flows to a turbine, which drives an electric generator. Power lines carry the electricity out of the facility.

Energy Independence in Brazil

The government of Brazil made a commitment in the 1970s to use ethanol derived from sugarcane as the nation's primary vehicle fuel. Today, most new automobiles made in Brazil are flex-fuel vehicles, which can run on either ethanol or gasoline. Because of this use of ethanol, together with its own supplies of petroleum, Brazil no longer had to import foreign oil by 2006.

Biomass

Material derived from living things can produce energy for heating buildings, fueling vehicles, and other uses. This material—called biomass—includes some items that are usually treated as waste, such as cornstalks, sawdust, scrap paper, spoiled grain, and tree limbs. In addition, some farmers grow crops such as corn, sugarcane, sugar beets, prairie grass, and fast-growing trees such as poplars to convert into energy.

Living plants remove carbon dioxide from the atmosphere during photosynthesis. When biomass is burned, it returns the same amount of carbon dioxide into the atmosphere. This means that the use of biomass for fuel does not cause an increase in greenhouse gas levels in the atmosphere. However, energy is less concentrated in biomass than it is in fossil fuels—so, for example, a car using biomass fuel has to fill up more often than a car using fossil fuel.

In 2006, there were more than 5 million flex-fuel vehicles on the road in the United States. Such cars and trucks have modified engines that allow them to run on either gasoline or ethanol. Ethanol is a type of fuel that can be made from corn, sugar, and other plant material. Ethanol fuel is produced using the same method used to produce alcoholic beverages—fermentation, in which sugars and starches are converted into ethyl alcohol and carbon dioxide.

The Energy Policy Act of 2005 set a goal of increasing U.S. production of ethanol fuel and other biomass fuels to 7.5 billion gallons (28 billion liters)

Fuel Cells

Another alternative energy source for transportation is the fuel cell. Fuel cells convert chemical energy from hydrogen gas or another fuel into electrical energy. Hybrid cars are vehicles that have both an internal combustion engine to burn gasoline and a fuel cell to produce electrical energy.

NUCLEAR AND RENEWABLE ENERGY

per year by 2012. The United States obtained approximately 3 percent of its energy from biomass in 2004.

Geothermal Power

The energy that causes the Old Faithful geyser in Yellowstone National Park to shoot hot water into the sky can also be converted into electrical power. Geothermal power comes from heat that is generated inside Earth. In volcanic areas around the world, magma (hot, partially melted rock) from deep inside the planet oozes upward and heats rocks and aquifers several miles below the surface, sometimes to temperatures greater than 570° Fahrenheit (300° Celsius).

Geothermal power plants use systems of pipes and pumps to draw the hot water or steam out of the ground and into an electrical power-generating device, such as a steam turbine. The water used by geothermal power plants is continually replenished when it rains.

A number of countries use geothermal power in limited amounts. It represented about 0.3 percent of the total U.S. energy consumption in 2004.

Wind Power

If you have ever flown a kite or traveled in a sailboat, you know how powerful the wind can be. Scientists have estimated that all of the wind in the world produces

Hot Power in Iceland

Iceland has several geothermal resources associated with a zone of underground volcanic activity that spreads across the country. Magma in this zone heats underground water to temperatures greater than 390°F (200°C), resulting in many hot springs and geysers. Many people in Iceland draw this hot water up with pumps and use it directly for space heating. Geothermal energy facilities convert this natural heat into electrical power. This geothermal power station (*right*) converts some of Iceland's natural underground heat into electrical power for industrial and residential use.

From Windmills to Wind Turbines

Denmark is a windy country that has used windmills to produce energy for many centuries. Within the past twenty-five years or so, Denmark has exploited the power of the wind more efficiently with thousands of wind turbines, which generate much of the country's electrical power. Many of Denmark's wind farms are located offshore, where strong winds turn large turbines to produce electricity.

more than 11 quadrillion kilowatt-hours of kinetic (movement) energy each year. A kilowatt-hour is a unit that represents the amount of work performed by 1,000 watts (units of electrical and mechanical power) every hour.

A traditional windmill uses the kinetic energy of the wind to turn a shaft, which then operates machinery to perform tasks such as pumping water or grinding grain. A modern wind turbine uses the same kind of rotational energy to drive electrical power generators. A wind turbine can convert about 40 percent of the wind's energy into electrical power. Wind power generated about 0.1 percent of U.S. energy in 2004.

Although wind power is a pollution-free, renewable source of energy, some people are opposed to its use for various reasons. For example, wind turbines harm birds that accidentally fly into them, and wind farms (large groups of wind turbines) produce loud noises.

Solar Power

We see how plants use the Sun's energy to grow. People can also use the energy from the Sun to produce electricity. Solar power currently plays only a small role in the world's energy production, but some-day—when more efficient ways are developed to use the Sun's energy—solar power might be the world's most important energy supplier.

Devices called photovoltaic cells are made of material (mainly silicon) that can easily conduct heat and electricity.

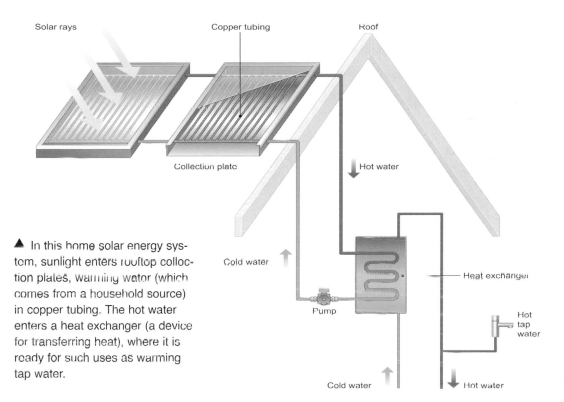

Solar rays   Copper tubing   Roof

Collection plate

Hot water

▲ In this home solar energy system, sunlight enters rooftop collection plates, warming water (which comes from a household source) in copper tubing. The hot water enters a heat exchanger (a device for transferring heat), where it is ready for such uses as warming tap water.

Cold water

Pump

Heat exchanger

Hot tap water

Cold water   Hot water

Energy from the Sun causes electric charges to flow through this material, producing electric currents. Many hand-held calculators and wristwatches, as well as spacecraft and satellites, use this type of solar energy.

Solar conversion systems use another type of solar energy. These systems often have rows of reflectors to focus sunlight onto fluid-filled pipes or collection plates. The fluid in the pipes or plates may reach temperatures greater than 750°F (400°C). This heat can be used to warm buildings and to make steam for the generation of electricity.

Solar Cooking Stoves

Solar cooking stoves are simple devices that can be built out of cardboard, aluminum foil, plastic, and other basic materials. These devices concentrate the Sun's rays onto pots in order to slowly cook food. You can cook vegetables, eggs, meat, pasta, and many other food items on solar cooking stoves.

Solar power accounted for only 0.06 percent of the total U.S. energy consumption in 2004. Some homes use solar energy, and some industries, such as the steel industry, use limited amounts of solar energy.

8 USING RESOURCES WISELY

From water to minerals to soil and fuels, the resources we consume place great demands on Earth. As the population of our planet grows, it is increasingly important to use Earth's natural resources wisely. We all need to conserve natural resources as much as possible in order to ensure that future generations will have a healthy, high-quality standard of living.

One important way we can conserve Earth's resources is through recycling. Many resources—such as paper, plastic, glass, aluminum, copper, steel, and motor oil—can be used more than once. After we use these products, they can be collected and recycled into new items for other people to use. This not only prolongs the use of Earth's resources but it also reduces the pollution that might result from disposing of the wastes.

You can take recyclable items to buy-back or drop-off centers in your area. More and more cities in the United States, however, have curbside collection programs in which homeowners simply deposit recyclables in special containers. Collectors then take the items to reprocessing facilities.

If good conservation practices are adopted, two goals will be achieved. Not only will the environment be protected for future generations, but high levels of productivity in agriculture and industry will also be maintained. Business leaders, government officials, scientists, and individual citizens are working together in communities across the United States and in other countries to find the best ways to achieve these goals.

Perhaps you, too, can become involved in these efforts. You can help conservation efforts in your community and practice conservation in your own home. Here is an easy-to-remember tip that might help you conserve resources: "reduce, reuse, and recycle." For example, you can reduce your use of paper products by using one paper towel instead of two to clean up a spill in the kitchen. Alternatively, you may want to use a reusable, washable cloth instead of a paper towel to clean up the spill. You might also be able to recycle both the paper towel and the cloth for other purposes, such as cleaning up dirty material in the garage. Keep "reduce, reuse, and recycle" in mind, and you will be surprised how far you can stretch resources—and how much you can save!

The natural resources of Earth provide us with everything we need. If we use them with care, respect, and intelligence, Earth's natural resources will always be with us as we live fulfilling, productive lives.

What is Your Ecological Footprint?

Your "ecological footprint" refers to the amount of natural resources you use and how your use of these resources affects the natural environment. Calculating ecological footprints is very complicated, but, according to some estimates, the average ecological footprint of a person living in the United States is thirteen times greater than that of a person living in India and fifty-two times greater than that of someone in Somalia.

▼ You can drop off cans, magazines, and a variety of other used materials at recycling centers. Your city or community may also have a collection program for recyclable items.

GLOSSARY

Btu British Thermal Unit, a unit used to measure heat; one Btu raises the temperature of 1 pound (0.454 kg) of water 1°F (0.556°C)

carbohydrate A chemical compound that contains oxygen, hydrogen, and carbon atoms

catalyst A substance that changes the rate of a chemical reaction, typically by speeding it up

crop rotation A system of growing a succession of different crops in a field to prevent the nutrients in the soil from becoming depleted

crust The rocky outer layer of Earth, including both the continents and the ocean floor

degradation The damage caused to soil in various ways, such as by being contaminated with salt or toxic chemicals

desertification The conversion of formerly fertile, productive land into infertile, barren land

DNA Deoxyribonucleic acid, the chainlike molecule that makes up genes, the units of heredity in cells

erosion The process by which rock and soil are broken loose from Earth's surface at one location and moved to another location

fermentation A chemical process that breaks down organic material, such as when yeast breaks down sugar into ethyl alcohol and carbon dioxide

fossil fuel Petroleum (crude oil), natural gas, and coal; fossil fuels are derived from the fossilized remains of plants, animals, and other organisms

geothermal Having to do with the internal heat of Earth

geyser A hot spring that ejects water with great force periodically

greenhouse gas A gas that allows sunlight to enter the atmosphere but traps some of the heat rays radiated by Earth's surface

hot spring A spring with water that is heated by natural processes within Earth

humus A dark brown substance in soil that is formed when dead plant and animal material decays

hydrocarbon A chemical compound containing only hydrogen and carbon

Industrial Revolution The change from an agriculture-based society to an industry-based society that took place in Europe and North America mainly in the 1800s

infrared Having to do with heat rays, a form of energy that is given off by any warm object

malleable Able to be hammered or pressed into various shapes without being broken

nucleus The core, or central part, of an atom, containing protons and neutrons

ore A mineral resource that contains enough metal to make it worth mining

organic Having to do with material that was produced by plant or animal activities

ozone A form of oxygen in which each molecule is made of three oxygen atoms, instead of the two atoms in "regular" oxygen

particulate A very small particle that makes up part of smog and other forms of air pollution

peat Partially decayed plant material that collects in swamps over long periods of time

photosynthesis The process in which light energy from the Sun is used by plants to combine carbon dioxide with water to make carbohydrates

radioactive Giving off energy in the form

of alpha, beta, or gamma rays because of the breaking up of atoms

respiration The process by which a plant, animal, or living cell obtains oxygen from the air or water and uses it to produce energy, giving off carbon dioxide in the process

RNA Ribonucleic acid, a molecule that helps the body produce proteins

salt dome A circular structure above the ground resulting from the upward movement of a mass of salt from below the ground

terracing The construction of several wide, flat rows of farmland on hillsides to help prevent soil erosion

tide The regular, recurring rise and fall of the water in oceans and large lakes, caused by the gravitational pull of the moon and Sun

turbine An engine or motor in which a wheel with vanes revolves because of the force of water, steam, or air; turbines are often used to power generators that produce electricity

water table Level below which the ground is saturated with water

weathering The destructive or discoloring action of air, water, or other natural factors on rock or wood

FURTHER INFORMATION

Books
Bartoletti, Susan C. *Growing Up in Coal Country*. Houghton, 1996.

Brown, Paul. *Global Pollution*. Raintree, 2003.

Daley, Michael J. *Nuclear Power*. Lerner Publications, 1997.

DuTemple, Lesley A. *Oil Spills*. Lucent Books, 1999.

Farndon, John. (*Science Experiments* series) *Rocks and Minerals*. Benchmark Books, 2003.

Stille, Darlene. *Soil: Digging Into Earth's Vital Resource*. Compass Point Books, 2005.

Trueit, Trudi S. *Rocks, Gems, and Minerals*. Watts, 2003.

Wilcox, Charlotte. *Powerhouse: Inside a Nuclear Power Plant*. Carolrhoda, 1996.

Web Sites
Energy Efficiency and Renewable Energy
www.eere.energy.gov

Energy Information Administration
www.eia.doe.gov

Mining Technology
www.mining-technology.com

Nuclear Energy Institute
www.nei.org

Sustainable Ecosystems Institute
www.sei.org

Sustainability Institute
www.sustainabilityinstitute.org

World Energy News
www.worldenergynews.com

DVDs
Empires of Industry–Black Gold: The Story of Oil. A&E Home Video, 2005.

Global Warming: The Signs and the Science. PBS Home Video, 2005.

History of Nuclear Energy: Problems and Promises. A2ZCDS.com, 2005.

INDEX